Dolphin Love

Dedicated to all the beautiful dolphins

and the dolphin in all of us.....

Dolphin Love

Sixty ways to live and love like a Dolphin

Chris and Sophie Michell

Calligraphy by Angela Swan

Cover painting by Marcus Burnett

Delphi Books

First published in Great Britain 1994
by

DELPHI BOOKS

ASTARTE MUSIC

P.O. BOX 875 BATH BA1 3TJ

Copyright © Chris and Sophie Michell 1994

ISBN 0-9524815-0-2

All rights reserved

Calligraphy by Angela Swan

Cover painting by Marcus Burnett

Printed and bound in Great Britain by
Redcliff Print & Design, 30 The Weir, Hessle, East Yorkshire HU13 ORU

Dolphin Love

is having fun, fun, fun

Dolphin Love
is letting go

Dolphin Love
is total unconditional
LOVE

Dolphin Love

is effortless

Dolphin Love

is having no fear

Dolphin Love

is dolphin smiles

Dolphin Love

is sharing the joy

Dolphin Love

is
a dive
in the
deep

Dolphin Love
is simply spontaneous

Dolphin Love

is deep, deep peace

Dolphin Love

is navigating the oceans of the mind

Dolphin Love

is
a big
heart
chakra

Dolphin Love

*is
realising
we are
all
ONE*

Dolphin Love

is flying above the clouds

Dolphin Love

is limitless freedom

Dolphin Love

is lightness of being

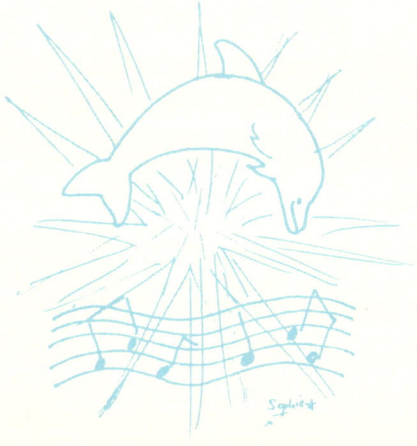

Dolphin Love

is frolicking in the blue

Dolphin Love

is
total
trust

Dolphin Love
is recognising a stranger

Dolphin Love

is a global pod

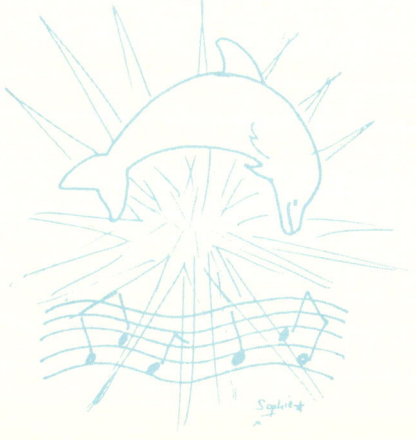

Dolphin Love

*is
mother
and
baby*

Dolphin Love

is a crystal star

Dolphin Love

is a phosphorescent twinkle

Dolphin Love

is the rhythm of the ocean

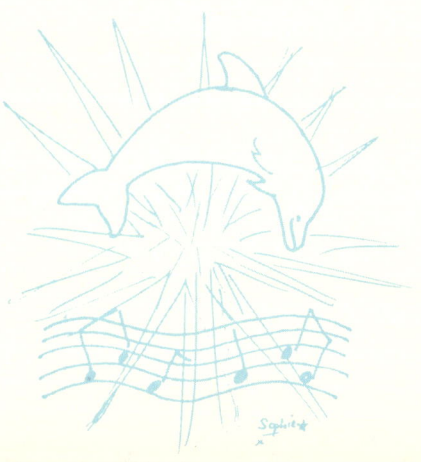

*Dolphin
Love*

*is
dancing
a dolphin
dance*

Dolphin Love

*is
riding
the crest
of a
wave*

Dolphin Love is frequently frivolous

Dolphin Love

*is
complete
honesty
and
openness*

Dolphin Love

is seeing the funny side of things

Dolphin Love
is purity of heart

Dolphin Love
*is the
silver sound
of the
flute*

Dolphin Love
needs no approval

Dolphin Love is non-judgemental

Dolphin Love

is freely given

Dolphin Love

is a warm caress

Dolphin Love

is a toothy grin

Dolphin Love

is making eye contact

Dolphin Love
is a helping hand

Dolphin Love

is having a great chat

Sophie

Dolphin Love

is
pure
emotion

Sophie

Dolphin Love
knows no boundaries

Dolphin Love

is cruising around

Dolphin Love

*is
interspecies,
interdimensional
communication*

Dolphin Love

is flirting freely

Dolphin Love

*is
being in
each
perfect
moment*

Dolphin Love

is orgasmic waves of energy

Dolphin Love

is when your heart LEAPS like a dolphin

Dolphin Love

is travelling through time

Dolphin Love

is finding a pearl in an oyster

Dolphin Love

is a kaleidoscope of colours

Dolphin Love
is
the stars
in the
Milky Way

Dolphin Love

is a rainbow on the horizon

Dolphin Love

is a silver lining to every cloud

Dolphin Love

*is
dappled
light
on the
sea bed*

Dolphin Love

is sunshine sparkling on the ocean

Sophiek
x

Dolphin Love
is quicksilver movement

Dolphin Love

is the
flash
of a fin
above
the surf

Dolphin Love

feels like the smooth wet velvet of a dolphin's skin

Dolphin Love
is the sheer JOY
of being alive

Chris and her daughter Sophie have travelled world-wide to swim with their dolphin friends and want to share the joyful dolphin lifestyle with you through this beautiful book

They are very concerned about the environmental threat to dolphins and whales and are contributing proceeds from the sale of this book to the
Whale and Dolphin Conservation Society

Membership and details of the society may be obtained from:

SEAN WHYTE
WDCS
Alexander House
James Street West
BATH BA1 2BT

Tel: 0225 334511